Master Time

Volume 2

Master Time

Volume 2

by Ace Doligosa

GOKUREN PUBLISHING
2021

Copyright © 2021 by Gokuren Publishing/ Ace Doligosa

For more
information, please
contact us at
Gokuren1984@gmail.com

Edited by Jordan Goldmeier
Cover Designed by Julie Horino
Formatting and layout by Julie Horino

First edition March 2021

ISBN 978-1-7356765-2-4-53599 (Hardback)

Dedicated to my mother, Evangeline Doligosa. Thank you for always believing in me and being saintly and patient with my growth. I am proud to call you my mother.

Table of Contents

Preface.. 11

Introduction 14

Vision and Goals 16

Month Plan 20

Week 1 24

Week 2 40

Week 3 56

Week 4 72

Week 5 89

Notes 104

About Author 113

Preface

This planner was inspired by an article I read called "How to Master Time." In this article, SGI President, Daisaku Ikeda, explains: "Everyone has the same 24 hours in a day. However, if you use those hours wisely, you can accomplish a week's worth of effort in a day, or 10 years worth of effort in a year. I have lived my life with that spirit." (Jan. 1, 2016, World Tribune, p. 8)

When I started writing this series, I planned on making a 12-book set to account for the 12 months of the year. The first volume of this series is designed for you to start at any time and jump right into any circumstance.

A lot happened during the pandemic: my car was towed & repossessed; the LA lockdown hit; my Mother contracted COVID-19 on the other side of the country in New York City; I was kicked out of my apartment; my plans to secure investment had to be postponed without a date in sight (This meant I had no income); I was facing creditors and I had no health insurance; and anxiety/waves of panic struck me every 5-10 minutes as I was leaving a toxic relationship. What kept me sane and afloat was my faith and my time management skills. What I learned during this tumultuous time in my life is that when we take care of our basic needs, little by little, our mind and emotions free up from the anxiety that clogs our lives, slowly but surely allowing us to advance and move forward.

When referring to Maslov's Hierarchy of needs, it's suggested that we take care of the bottom than grow to the top… based on what I went through during the COVID-19 Pandemic, I disagree. I believe it starts with the hope that we can be and do better. Our desires and emotions are the inertia we need to take our first steps. When we decide to do this, our desires and emotions become the internal inertia we need to take our first step. Our behaviors shift and therefore our circumstances begin to transform from moment to moment.

THE 6 HUMAN NEEDS

Now that we have established what this book is about, let us talk about how to use it. Below are the 6 Human Needs:

By Tony Robbins

1. **Certainty**: assurance you can avoid pain and gain pleasure
2. **Uncertainty/Variety**: the need for the unknown, change, new stimuli
3. **Significance**: feeling unique, important, special or needed
4. **Connection/Love**: a strong feeling of closeness or union with someone or something
5. **Growth**: an expansion of capacity, capability or understanding
6. **Contribution**: a sense of service and focus on helping, giving to and supporting others

Below I have described a task, then mapped the basic need and finally wrote the purpose and result. In this way, I have traced my activities to fulfilling my needs. By writing the result, I make my needs crystal clear.

MASTER TIME BREAKDOWN

Task	Need Addressed	Purpose & Result
Fill Out Weekly Plan On Sunday	Certainty	Eliminate feelings of anxiety for your week & end the dread of Monday morning
Fill Out Weekly/Daily Workout Plans	Steady growth & self-built significance	Build cumulative physical and mental strength
Plan three activities for fun	Uncertainty, variety	Without variety, routines become mundane and stifling. Opening up room for variety opens your mind and heart to new waves of thought and inspiration
Call three people a day	Connection, Love, significance	With the right network - mitigate loneliness, curb habits of talking longer than you feel like you should
Answer "What day is it?"	Certainty, catharsis	Center and stable yourself in the present
List three things to be grateful for	Certainty, Contribution	Enabling more gratitude into your life lessens anxiety, arrogance, impatience, and entitlement, allowing more space in your life for happiness and progression

Task	Need Addressed	Purpose & Result
Task list	Certainty, clarity	Get out all the stuff in your head you're worried about forgetting and put it somewhere useful. Once you relieve your mind of these nagging tasks, you'll feel more peace
Write down one person you appreciate and why	Connection, love, significance	When we appreciate others for who they are or what they have done, we shift from blaming others to appreciating others and ourselves
Schedule your meal times	Basic human need, we must eat food or we'll die	Take control of your eating habits. The better we plan and regiment our food intake, the better we can nourish and take care of our bodies
Develop your belief systems	Certainty, uncertainty	A single belief has the power to save your life or that of others. A strong system enhances trust in yourself and your own capabilities
Schedule work time	Certainty, contribution, growth	Doing work can seem dreadful until we schedule the right amount of time for us to do it. Then we do it and that looming dread is exchanged with fulfillment as we accomplish each task within a designated block of time
Overview	Certainty, cognition, growth	After you build out each block of your day, re-organizing and re-writing each block in the larger overview cements each time block to memory. Eventually, you won't need to carry the book around and the tasks will stick to memory

Having mastered Volume, you are now ready for the next step along your journey.

Introduction

Let's talk about Volume 2

Now that you have started a new life rhythm that balances your needs using Volume 1, Volume 2 expands more on your vision and gives space for reflection.

What worked from last month? What didn't work?

As we grow, our vision for ourselves begins to clear up and there is room for us to work on the granular details. The more specific we are in building our vision and the more open we are to adjusting and upgrading specific aspects of our lives, the stronger and more confident we truly become.

In this volume, the daily and weekly framework hasn't changed but the vision and reflection spaces have developed.

Vision and Goals

You made it! Describe your vision of success for yourself in *30 years*. Take some time to imagine it and write it down here.

What is your definition of success?

When you have made it, who is by your side?

What are the newspapers saying about your success story?

What does it feel like?

Where are you living?

Who have you paid back?

What promises have you kept?

Who have you made proud?

Describe the following parts of your life

Relationships / Social
Now:

In 30 years:

Career
Now:

In 30 years:

Finances
Now:

In 30 years:

Love
Now:

In 30 years:

Home life
Now:

In 30 years:

Recreational / Hobbies
Now:

In 30 years:

Why do you deserve your dream (What impact will you make while you are achieving your dream?)

Name 5 reasons:

1.

2.

3.

4.

5.

Are my current behaviors and habits aligned with my life vision? (Seriously...?)

What are the milestones to get there? (Have they changed since last month?)

What are your 3-year goals towards this dream?

Answer from Volume 1	New Answer

Think bigger...

What are your 5-year goals towards this dream?

Answer from Volume 1 | New Answer

What are your 10-year goals towards this dream?

Answer from Volume 1 | New Answer

What are your 30-year goals towards this dream?

Answer from Volume 1 | New Answer

	SUN	MON	TUE

WED	THU	FRI	SAT

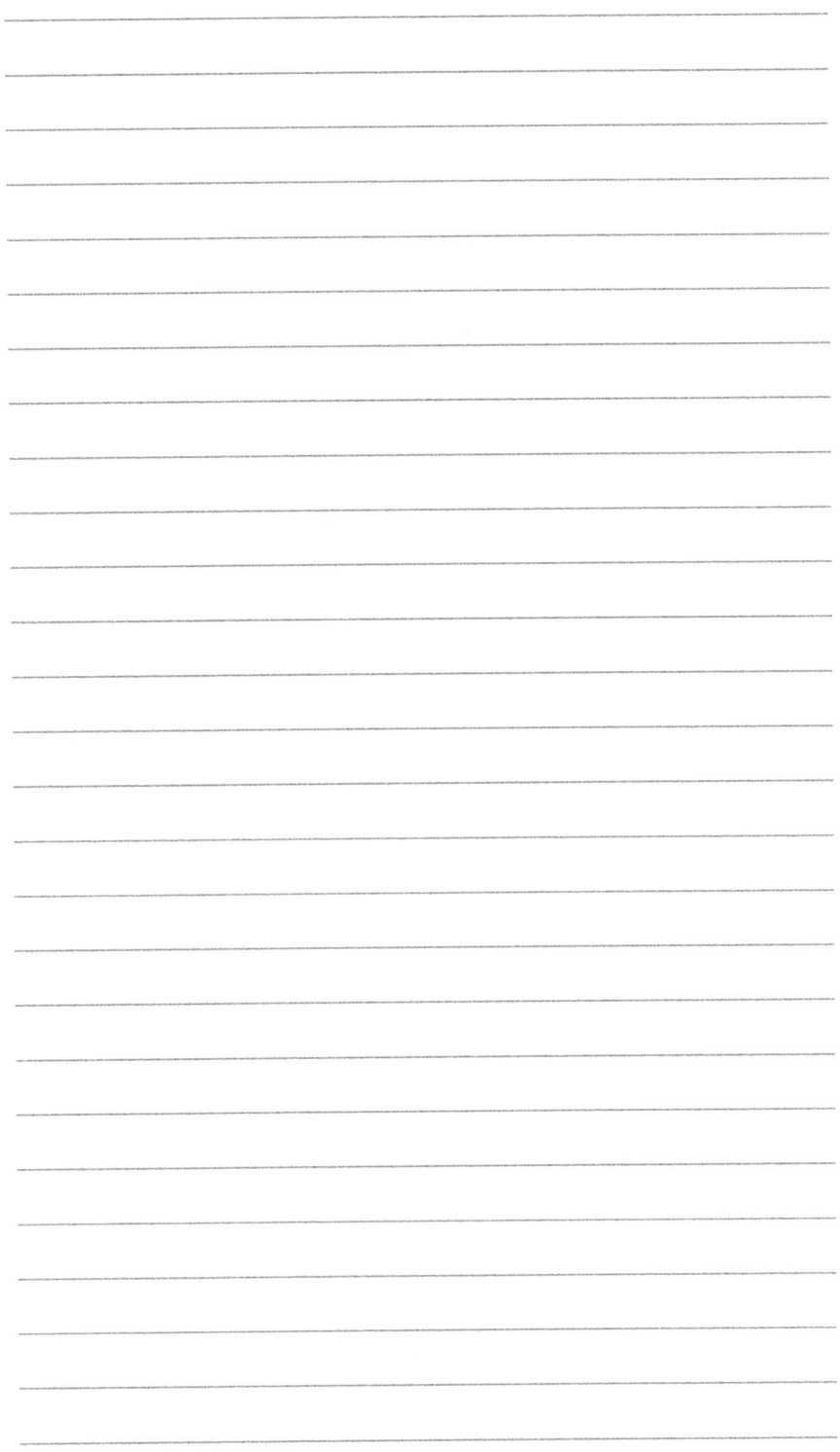

> *"Start over my darling. Be brave enough to chase it. Then start over and love yourself the way you were always meant to."*
> *- Madalyn Beck*

1. 45-Minute Daily conditioning workouts to keep you feeling strong

SUN	MON	TUE	WED	THU	FRI	SAT

2. Plan 3 calls each day to feel connected and mitigate the risk of isolation & depression

SUN	MON	TUE	WED	THU	FRI	SAT

3. Plan 3 activities a week for fun

SUN	MON	TUE	WED	THU	FRI	SAT

Pro-tip:

Joan Rivers once said, "I allow myself a 48 hour pity day." When things go wrong and you need some time to mourn or sort out your emotions, take the time. It is more important for you and the people around you to resolve anything that must be resolved. Only bad things happen when you ignore your emotions, clarity happens when you brave them. Give yourself time to go through any emotions you need to. This is the greatest gift you could ever give the world.

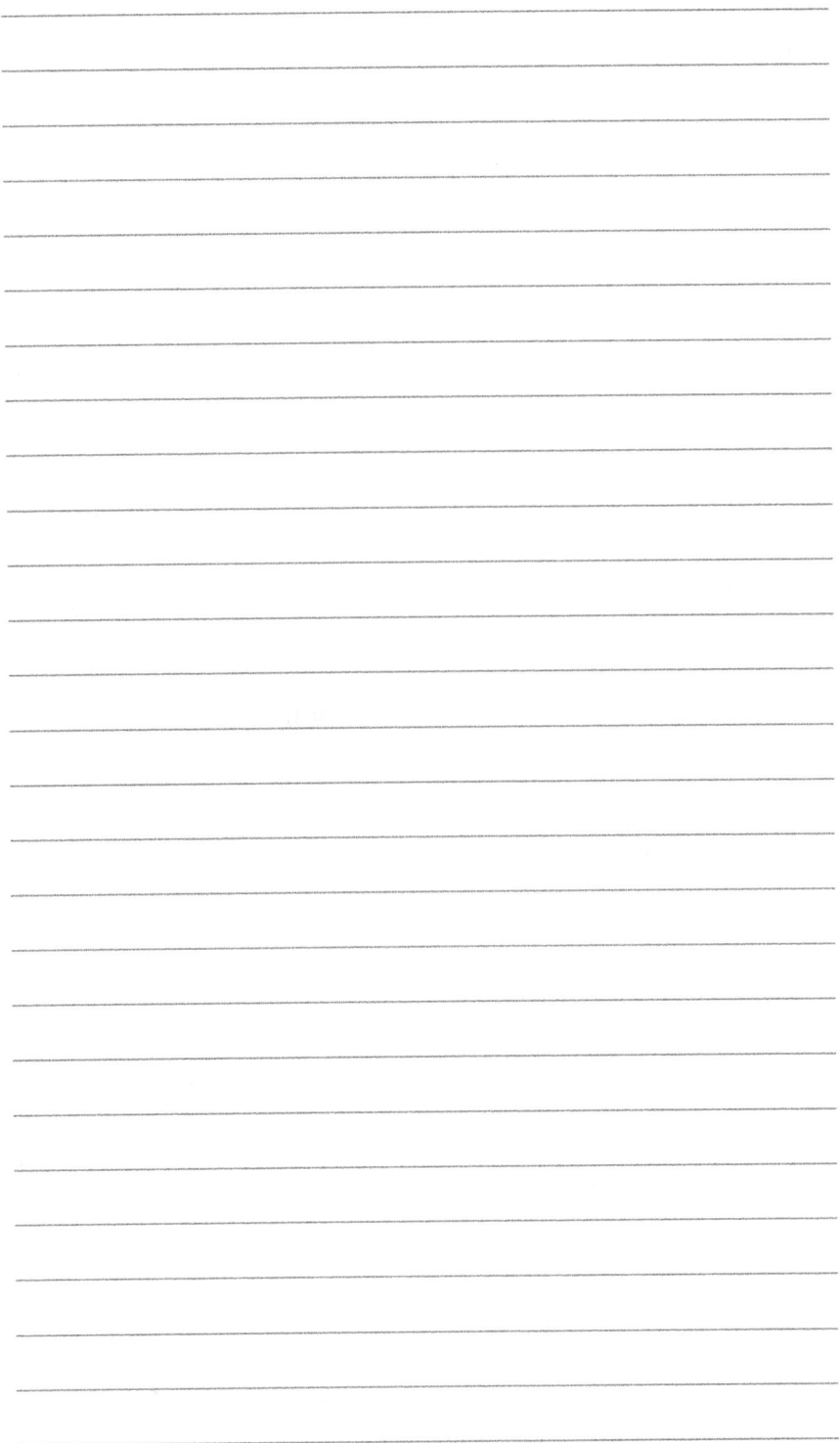

What day is it? ....

> ### *"It's possible to choose your future."*
> ### *- Les Brown*

List 3 things you are
grateful for...

- _____
- _____
- _____

List 3-10 tasks you must
accomplish today...

- _____
- _____
- _____
- _____
- _____
- _____
- _____
- _____
- _____
- _____

Schedule your meal times...

- ___ : ___ ~ ___ : ___
- ___ : ___ ~ ___ : ___
- ___ : ___ ~ ___ : ___
- ___ : ___ ~ ___ : ___
- ___ : ___ ~ ___ : ___

Find 2 hours for metaphysics / belief
system development...

- ___ : ___ ~ ___ : ___
- ___ : ___ ~ ___ : ___
- ___ : ___ ~ ___ : ___
- ___ : ___ ~ ___ : ___
- ___ : ___ ~ ___ : ___
- ___ : ___ ~ ___ : ___

Who do you appreciate today?

> *"A man cannot directly choose his circumstances, but he can choose his thoughts, and so indirectly, yet surely, shape his circumstances."*
> *- James Allen*

Schedule workouts...

1. 10-minute Cardio

_____

2. 10-minute Stretch

_____

3. 25-minute Activity

_____

Schedule work time...

When are your meetings for today?

:   ~   :   •

:   ~   :   • _____

:   ~   :   • _____

:   ~   :   • _____

:   ~   :   •

Carry over tasks...

Overview
What does today look like?

:   ~   : _____

:   ~   : _____

:   ~   : _____

:   ~   : _____

:   ~   : _____

:   ~   : _____

:   ~   : _____

:   ~   : _____

:   ~   : _____

:   ~   : _____

:   ~   : _____

:   ~   : _____

What day is it?

> "Another thing I did to deflect the course of my thoughts was to listen to my heart."
> - Albert Camus

List 3 things you are grateful for...

- _____
- _____
- _____

List 3-10 tasks you must accomplish today...

- _____
- _____
- _____
- _____
- _____
- _____
- _____
- _____
- _____
- _____

Schedule your meal times...

: ~ : •
: ~ : •
: ~ : •
: ~ : •
: ~ : •

Find 2 hours for metaphysics / belief system development...

: ~ : •
: ~ : •
: ~ : •
: ~ : •
: ~ : •
: ~ : •

Who do you appreciate today?

> *"If a young person does not learn to inspire trust in others, failure is almost certain."*
> *- Daisaku Ikeda*

Schedule workouts...

1. 10-minute Cardio

_____

2. 10-minute Stretch

_____

3. 25-minute Activity

_____

Schedule work time...

When are your meetings for today?

  : ~ : •
_____
  : ~ : •
_____
  : ~ : •
_____
  : ~ : •
_____
  : ~ : •

Carry over tasks...

Overview
What does today look like?

: ~ :
: ~ :
: ~ :
: ~ :
: ~ :
: ~ :
: ~ :
: ~ :
: ~ :
: ~ :
: ~ :
: ~ :

What day is it?

> *"It's true how our own relationship with death can give us strength."*
> *- Ace Doligosa*

List 3 things you are grateful for...

- _____
- _____
- _____

List 3-10 tasks you must accomplish today...

- _____
- _____
- _____
- _____
- _____
- _____
- _____
- _____
- _____
- _____

Schedule your meal times...

:   ~   :   • _____
:   ~   :   • _____
:   ~   :   • _____
:   ~   :   • _____
:   ~   :   • _____

Find 2 hours for metaphysics / belief system development...

:   ~   :   • _____
:   ~   :   • _____
:   ~   :   • _____
:   ~   :   • _____
:   ~   :   • _____
:   ~   :   • _____

Who do you appreciate today?

"Why are you here?"
- Les Brown

Schedule workouts...

1. 10-minute Cardio

_____

2. 10-minute Stretch

_____

3. 25-minute Activity

_____

Schedule work time...

When are your meetings for today?

: ~ : • _____

: ~ : • _____

: ~ : • _____

: ~ : • _____

: ~ : • _____

Carry over tasks...

Overview
What does today look like?

: ~ : _____

: ~ : _____

: ~ : _____

: ~ : _____

: ~ : _____

: ~ : _____

: ~ : _____

: ~ : _____

: ~ : _____

: ~ : _____

: ~ : _____

: ~ : _____

What day is it? _____

List 3 things you are grateful for...

- _____
- _____
- _____

List 3-10 tasks you must accomplish today...

- _____
- _____
- _____
- _____
- _____
- _____
- _____
- _____
- _____
- _____

Schedule your meal times...

: ~ : • _____
: ~ : • _____
: ~ : • _____
: ~ : • _____
: ~ : • _____

Find 2 hours for metaphysics / belief system development...

: ~ : • _____
: ~ : • _____
: ~ : • _____
: ~ : • _____
: ~ : • _____
: ~ : • _____

Who do you appreciate today?

> *"If you know the why for doing, you can endure almost any how."*
> *- Nietzsche*

Schedule workouts...

1. 10-minute Cardio

_____

2. 10-minute Stretch

_____

3. 25-minute Activity

_____

Schedule work time...

When are your meetings for today?

: ~ :   •

: ~ :   • _____

: ~ :   • _____

: ~ :   • _____

: ~ :   •

Carry over tasks...

Overview
What does today look like?

: ~ :   _____

: ~ :   _____

: ~ :   _____

: ~ :   _____

: ~ :   _____

: ~ :   _____

: ~ :   _____

: ~ :   _____

: ~ :   _____

: ~ :   _____

: ~ :   _____

: ~ :   _____

What day is it?

> *"Family is not who's blood is in you, it's who you love and who loves you."*
> *- Jackie Chan*

List 3 things you are grateful for...

- _____
- _____
- _____

List 3-10 tasks you must accomplish today...

- _____
- _____
- _____
- _____
- _____
- _____
- _____
- _____
- _____
- _____

Schedule your meal times...

: ~ : •
: ~ : •
: ~ : •
: ~ : •
: ~ : •

Find 2 hours for metaphysics / belief system development...

: ~ : •
: ~ : •
: ~ : •
: ~ : •
: ~ : •
: ~ : •

Who do you appreciate today?

"No man, however grand, knows what he wants until you give it to him."
- Le Notre

Schedule workouts...

1. 10-minute Cardio

_____

2. 10-minute Stretch

_____

3. 25-minute Activity

_____

Schedule work time...

When are your meetings for today?

```
:   ~   :   •
:   ~   :   •   _____
:   ~   :   •   _____
:   ~   :   •   _____
:   ~   :   •
```

Carry over tasks...

Overview
What does today look like?

```
:   ~   :   _____
:   ~   :   _____
:   ~   :   _____
:   ~   :   _____
:   ~   :   _____
:   ~   :   _____
:   ~   :   _____
:   ~   :   _____
:   ~   :   _____
:   ~   :   _____
:   ~   :   _____
:   ~   :   _____
```

What day is it? _____

> ## "Respect the young."
> ### - Confucius

List 3 things you are grateful for...

- _____
- _____
- _____

List 3-10 tasks you must accomplish today...

- _____
- _____
- _____
- _____
- _____
- _____
- _____
- _____
- _____
- _____

Schedule your meal times...

- : ~ : •
- : ~ : • _____
- : ~ : • _____
- : ~ : • _____
- : ~ : • _____

Find 2 hours for metaphysics / belief system development...

- : ~ : •
- : ~ : • _____
- : ~ : • _____
- : ~ : • _____
- : ~ : • _____
- : ~ : • _____

Who do you appreciate today?

> "Everybody's a genius. But if you judge a fish by its ability to climb a tree,
> it will live its whole life believing that it's stupid."
> - Albert Einstein

Schedule workouts...

1. 10-minute Cardio

_____

2. 10-minute Stretch

_____

3. 25-minute Activity

_____

Schedule work time...

When are your meetings for today?

: ~ : •
_____
: ~ : •
_____
: ~ : •
_____
: ~ : •
_____
: ~ : •

Carry over tasks...

Overview
What does today look like?

: ~ :
_____
: ~ :
_____
: ~ :
_____
: ~ :
_____
: ~ :
_____
: ~ :
_____
: ~ :
_____
: ~ :
_____
: ~ :
_____
: ~ :
_____
: ~ :
_____
: ~ :

What day is it? ....

> *"There is always light, if only we're brave enough to see it;*
> *if only we're brave enough to be it."*
> *- Amanda Gorman*

List 3 things you are grateful for...

- _____
- _____
- _____

List 3-10 tasks you must accomplish today...

- _____
- _____
- _____
- _____
- _____
- _____
- _____
- _____
- _____
- _____

Schedule your meal times...

: ~ : •
: ~ : •
: ~ : •
: ~ : •
: ~ : •

Find 2 hours for metaphysics / belief system development...

: ~ : •
: ~ : •
: ~ : •
: ~ : •
: ~ : •
: ~ : •

Who do you appreciate today?

> *"The best advice I received from someone at a poker table was 'they're just chips. There's no value in them unless you put value in them.'"*
> *- Ace Doligosa*

Schedule workouts...

1. 10-minute Cardio

_____

2. 10-minute Stretch

_____

3. 25-minute Activity

_____

Schedule work time...

When are your meetings for today?

```
:   ~   :    •
:   ~   :    •  _____
:   ~   :    •  _____
:   ~   :    •  _____
:   ~   :    •
```

Carry over tasks...

Overview
What does today look like?

```
:   ~   :    _____
:   ~   :    _____
:   ~   :    _____
:   ~   :    _____
:   ~   :    _____
:   ~   :    _____
:   ~   :    _____
:   ~   :    _____
:   ~   :    _____
:   ~   :    _____
:   ~   :    _____
```

Weekly Plan

> "No one is such a coward that he could not be inspired into courage by love, and made the equal of someone who's naturally very brave."
> - Plato

1. 45-Minute Daily conditioning workouts to keep you feeling sharp

SUN	MON	TUE	WED	THU	FRI	SAT

2. Plan 3 calls a day to sustain your relationships

SUN	MON	TUE	WED	THU	FRI	SAT

3. Plan 3 activities a week for fun

SUN	MON	TUE	WED	THU	FRI	SAT

Pro-tip:

Keep asking *why*. This will allow you to unearth the false and limiting beliefs within you. Once you recognize these beliefs for what they are, you can change them into truth.

What day is it?

List 3 things you are grateful for...

- _____
- _____
- _____

List 3-10 tasks you must accomplish today...

- _____
- _____
- _____
- _____
- _____
- _____
- _____
- _____
- _____
- _____

Schedule your meal times...

:   ~   :   •
:   ~   :   •
:   ~   :   •
:   ~   :   •
:   ~   :   •

Find 2 hours for metaphysics / belief system development...

:   ~   :   •
:   ~   :   •
:   ~   :   •
:   ~   :   •
:   ~   :   •
:   ~   :   •

Who do you appreciate today?

> *"The goal is not to be better than other people but to be better than our previous selves."*
> *- The Dalai Lama*

Schedule workouts...

1. 10-minute Cardio

_____

2. 10-minute Stretch

_____

3. 25-minute Activity

_____

Schedule work time...

When are your meetings for today?

: ~ : •

: ~ : • _____

: ~ : • _____

: ~ : • _____

: ~ : • _____

Carry over tasks...

Overview
What does today look like?

: ~ : _____

: ~ : _____

: ~ : _____

: ~ : _____

: ~ : _____

: ~ : _____

: ~ : _____

: ~ : _____

: ~ : _____

: ~ : _____

: ~ : _____

: ~ : _____

: ~ : _____

What day is it?

List 3 things you are grateful for...

- _____
- _____
- _____

List 3-10 tasks you must accomplish today...

- _____
- _____
- _____
- _____
- _____
- _____
- _____
- _____
- _____
- _____

Schedule your meal times...

: ~ : •
: ~ : •
: ~ : •
: ~ : •
: ~ : •

Find 2 hours for metaphysics / belief system development...

: ~ : •
: ~ : •
: ~ : •
: ~ : •
: ~ : •
: ~ : •

Who do you appreciate today?

> *"All others are my teachers."*
> *- Eiji Yoshikawa*

Schedule workouts...

1. 10-minute Cardio

_____

2. 10-minute Stretch

_____

3. 25-minute Activity

_____

Schedule work time...

When are your meetings for today?

:   ~   :   •
_____

:   ~   :   •
_____

:   ~   :   •
_____

:   ~   :   •
_____

:   ~   :   •

Carry over tasks...

Overview
What does today look like?

:   ~   :
_____

:   ~   :
_____

:   ~   :
_____

:   ~   :
_____

:   ~   :
_____

:   ~   :
_____

:   ~   :
_____

:   ~   :
_____

:   ~   :
_____

:   ~   :
_____

:   ~   :
_____

:   ~   :
_____

What day is it? ....

> *"You know, psychologically speaking, vengeance rarely brings the catharsis we hope for."*
>
> *- Harley Quinn*

List 3 things you are grateful for...

- _____
- _____
- _____

List 3-10 tasks you must accomplish today...

- _____
- _____
- _____
- _____
- _____
- _____
- _____
- _____
- _____
- _____

Schedule your meal times...

: ~ : • _____

: ~ : • _____

: ~ : • _____

: ~ : • _____

: ~ : • _____

Find 2 hours for metaphysics / belief system development...

: ~ : • _____

: ~ : • _____

: ~ : • _____

: ~ : • _____

: ~ : • _____

: ~ : • _____

Who do you appreciate today?

> *"This life is like a dream. One cannot be sure that one will live until tomorrow."*
> *- Nichiren Daishonin*

Schedule workouts...

1. 10-minute Cardio

_____

2. 10-minute Stretch

_____

3. 25-minute Activity

_____

Schedule work time...

When are your meetings for today?

: ~ : •
: ~ : •
: ~ : •
: ~ : •
: ~ : •

Carry over tasks...

Overview
What does today look like?

: ~ :
: ~ :
: ~ :
: ~ :
: ~ :
: ~ :
: ~ :
: ~ :
: ~ :
: ~ :
: ~ :
: ~ :

What day is it?

List 3 things you are grateful for...

- _____
- _____
- _____

List 3-10 tasks you must accomplish today...

- _____
- _____
- _____
- _____
- _____
- _____
- _____
- _____
- _____
- _____

Schedule your meal times...

:   ~   :   • _____
:   ~   :   • _____
:   ~   :   • _____
:   ~   :   • _____
:   ~   :   • _____

Find 2 hours for metaphysics / belief system development...

:   ~   :   • _____
:   ~   :   • _____
:   ~   :   • _____
:   ~   :   • _____
:   ~   :   • _____
:   ~   :   • _____

Who do you appreciate today?

> *"The road of a pioneer is always difficult. But once you have built the road, others will join you."*
> *- Shin'ichi Yamamoto*

Schedule workouts...

1. 10-minute Cardio

_____

2. 10-minute Stretch

_____

3. 25-minute Activity

_____

Schedule work time...

When are your meetings for today?

:   ~   :   •
_____
:   ~   :   •
_____
:   ~   :   •
_____
:   ~   :   •
_____
:   ~   :   •

Carry over tasks...

Overview
What does today look like?

:   ~   :   _____
:   ~   :   _____
:   ~   :   _____
:   ~   :   _____
:   ~   :   _____
:   ~   :   _____
:   ~   :   _____
:   ~   :   _____
:   ~   :   _____
:   ~   :   _____
:   ~   :   _____

What day is it? _____

> *"If we cannot feel hope, it is time to create some."*
> *- Daisaku Ikeda*

List 3 things you are grateful for...

- _____
- _____
- _____

List 3-10 tasks you must accomplish today...

- _____
- _____
- _____
- _____
- _____
- _____
- _____
- _____
- _____
- _____

Schedule your meal times...

- : ~ : •
- : ~ : •
- : ~ : •
- : ~ : •
- : ~ : •

Find 2 hours for metaphysics / belief system development...

- : ~ : •
- : ~ : •
- : ~ : •
- : ~ : •
- : ~ : •
- : ~ : •

Who do you appreciate today?

> *"In the moments that you feel lost and you feel like you're at your lowest, there is always hope to be found if you have the courage to believe it."*
> *- Ace Doligosa*

Schedule workouts...

1. 10-minute Cardio

_____

2. 10-minute Stretch

_____

3. 25-minute Activity

_____

Schedule work time...

When are your meetings for today?

: ~ : •

: ~ : • _____

: ~ : • _____

: ~ : • _____

: ~ : •

Carry over tasks...

Overview
What does today look like?

: ~ : _____

: ~ : _____

: ~ : _____

: ~ : _____

: ~ : _____

: ~ : _____

: ~ : _____

: ~ : _____

: ~ : _____

: ~ : _____

: ~ : _____

: ~ : _____

What day is it?

List 3 things you are
grateful for...

• _____

• _____

• _____

List 3-10 tasks you must
accomplish today...

• _____

• _____

• _____

• _____

• _____

• _____

• _____

• _____

• _____

• _____

Schedule your meal times

: ~ : •

: ~ : •

: ~ : •

: ~ : •

: ~ : •

Find 2 hours for metaphysics / belief
system development...

: ~ : •

: ~ : •

: ~ : •

: ~ : •

: ~ : •

: ~ : •

Who do you appreciate today?

52

> *"Trust is a peculiar resource; it is built rather than depleted by use."*
> *- Unknown*

Schedule workouts...

1. 10-minute Cardio

_____

2. 10-minute Stretch

_____

3. 25-minute Activity

_____

Schedule work time...

When are your meetings for today?

: ~ : •
_____
: ~ : •
_____
: ~ : •
_____
: ~ : •
_____
: ~ : •

Carry over tasks...

Overview
What does today look like?

: ~ : _____
: ~ : _____
: ~ : _____
: ~ : _____
: ~ : _____
: ~ : _____
: ~ : _____
: ~ : _____
: ~ : _____
: ~ : _____
: ~ : _____
: ~ : _____

What day is it? _____

> *"A true friend never misunderstands you, no matter what you say."*
> *- Unknown*

List 3 things you are grateful for...

- _____
- _____
- _____

List 3-10 tasks you must accomplish today...

- _____
- _____
- _____
- _____
- _____
- _____
- _____
- _____
- _____
- _____

Schedule your meal times...

- : ~ : • _____
- : ~ : • _____
- : ~ : • _____
- : ~ : • _____
- : ~ : • _____

Find 2 hours for metaphysics / belief system development...

- : ~ : • _____
- : ~ : • _____
- : ~ : • _____
- : ~ : • _____
- : ~ : • _____
- : ~ : • _____

Who do you appreciate today?

> *"Because here's a sneaky truth about life. There's no such thing as not giving a fuck."*
> *- Mark Manson*

Schedule workouts...

1. 10-minute Cardio

_____

2. 10-minute Stretch

_____

3. 25-minute Activity

_____

Schedule work time...

When are your meetings for today?

: ~ : •
: ~ : • _____
: ~ : • _____
: ~ : • _____
: ~ : •

Carry over tasks...

Overview
What does today look like?

: ~ : _____
: ~ : _____
: ~ : _____
: ~ : _____
: ~ : _____
: ~ : _____
: ~ : _____
: ~ : _____
: ~ : _____
: ~ : _____
: ~ : _____
: ~ : _____
: ~ : _____

Weekly Plan

> *"How are you going to get closer to taking over the world this week?"*
> *- Jordan Goldmeier*

1. 45-Minute Daily conditioning workouts to keep you feeling sharp

SUN	MON	TUE	WED	THU	FRI	SAT

2. Plan 3 calls a day to sustain your relationships

SUN	MON	TUE	WED	THU	FRI	SAT

3. Plan 3 activities a week for fun

SUN	MON	TUE	WED	THU	FRI	SAT

Pro-tip:

Mark Manson once said, "You must give a fuck about something. It's part of our biology to always care about something and therefore to always give a fuck." Inspired by these words, answer this question for yourself: *What do you give a fuck about? What are you choosing to give a fuck about? And how can I not give a fuck about what ultimately does not matter?*

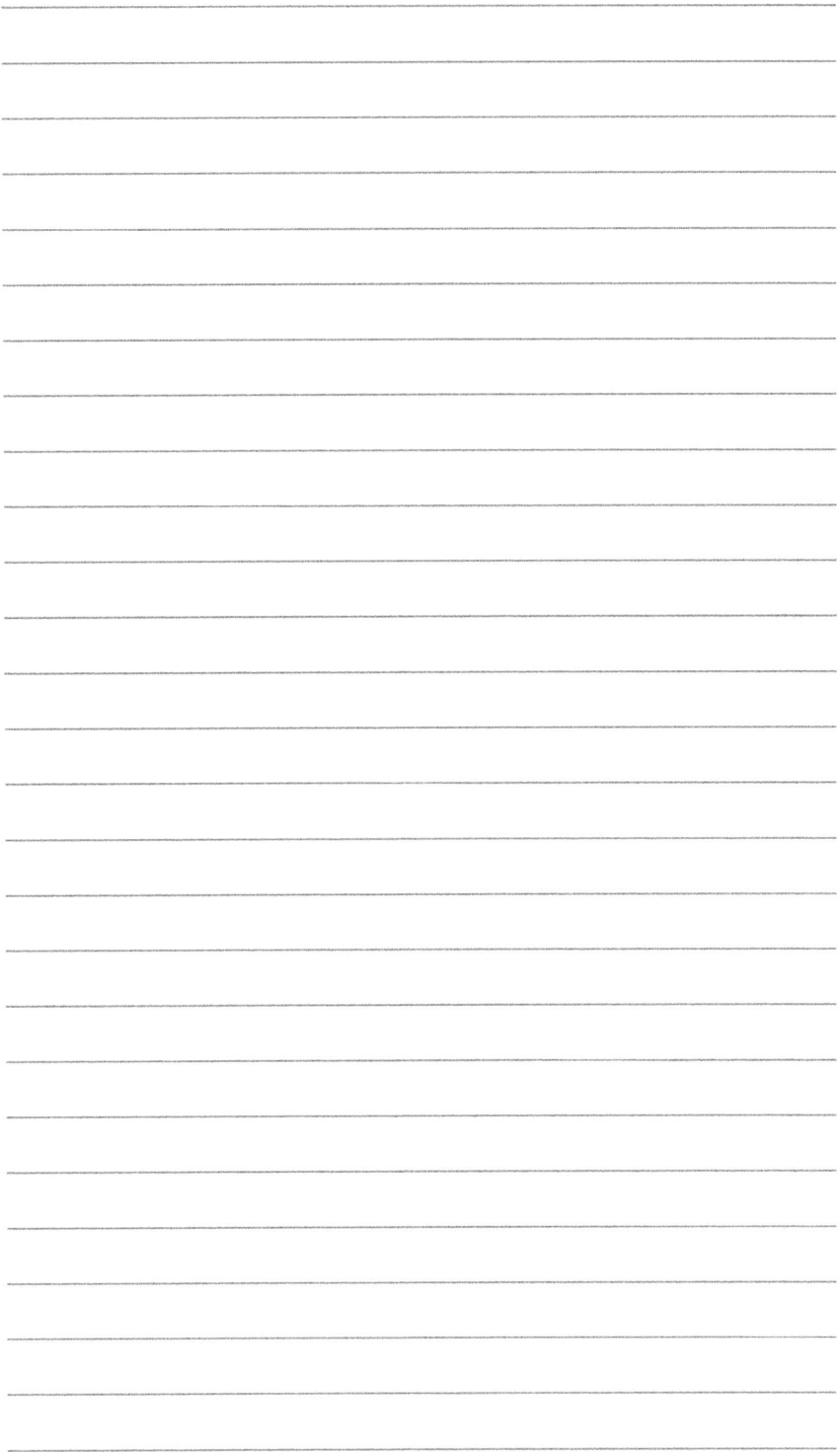

What day is it? _____

List 3 things you are grateful for...

- _____
- _____
- _____

List 3-10 tasks you must accomplish today...

- _____
- _____
- _____
- _____
- _____
- _____
- _____
- _____
- _____
- _____

Schedule your meal times...

:   ~   :   • _____

:   ~   :   • _____

:   ~   :   • _____

:   ~   :   • _____

:   ~   :   • _____

Find 2 hours for metaphysics / belief system development...

:   ~   :   • _____

:   ~   :   • _____

:   ~   :   • _____

:   ~   :   • _____

:   ~   :   • _____

:   ~   :   • _____

Who do you appreciate today?

> *"Who best can suffer, best can do. "*
> *- John Milton*

Schedule workouts...

1. 10-minute Cardio

_____

2. 10-minute Stretch

_____

3. 25-minute Activity

_____

Schedule work time...

When are your meetings for today?

:   ~   :   •
:   ~   :   • _____
:   ~   :   • _____
:   ~   :   • _____
:   ~   :   •

Carry over tasks...

Overview
What does today look like?

:   ~   : _____
:   ~   : _____
:   ~   : _____
:   ~   : _____
:   ~   : _____
:   ~   : _____
:   ~   : _____
:   ~   : _____
:   ~   : _____
:   ~   : _____
:   ~   : _____
:   ~   : _____

What day is it?

List 3 things you are grateful for...

- _____
- _____
- _____

Schedule your meal times...

: ~ : • _____
: ~ : • _____
: ~ : • _____
: ~ : • _____
: ~ : • _____

List 3-10 tasks you must accomplish today...

- _____
- _____
- _____
- _____
- _____
- _____
- _____
- _____
- _____
- _____

Find 2 hours for metaphysics / belief system development...

: ~ : • _____
: ~ : • _____
: ~ : • _____
: ~ : • _____
: ~ : • _____
: ~ : • _____

Who do you appreciate today?

> *"All things must be dealt with and now is the time to begin."*
> *- Brendon Burchard*

Schedule workouts...

1. 10-minute Cardio

_____

2. 10-minute Stretch

_____

3. 25-minute Activity

_____

Schedule work time...

When are your meetings for today?

```
:   ~   :   •
:   ~   :   •   _____
:   ~   :   •   _____
:   ~   :   •   _____
:   ~   :   •
```

Carry over tasks...

Overview
What does today look like?

```
:   ~   :   _____
:   ~   :   _____
:   ~   :   _____
:   ~   :   _____
:   ~   :   _____
:   ~   :   _____
:   ~   :   _____
:   ~   :   _____
:   ~   :   _____
:   ~   :   _____
:   ~   :   _____
```

What day is it?

> *"I've heard people say to themselves that they are broken... and at times parts of us can be but the best parts of us can never be broken. The best parts of us are stronger than any evil we have to face."*
> *- Ace Doligosa*

List 3 things you are grateful for...

- _____
- _____
- _____

List 3-10 tasks you must accomplish today...

- _____
- _____
- _____
- _____
- _____
- _____
- _____
- _____
- _____
- _____

Schedule your meal times...

:   ~   :   •
:   ~   :   •
:   ~   :   •
:   ~   :   •
:   ~   :   •

Find 2 hours for metaphysics / belief system development...

:   ~   :   •
:   ~   :   •
:   ~   :   •
:   ~   :   •
:   ~   :   •
:   ~   :   •

Who do you appreciate today?

"If it ain't broke, don't fix it."
- Bert Lance

Schedule workouts...

1. 10-minute Cardio

_____

2. 10-minute Stretch

_____

3. 25-minute Activity

_____

Schedule work time...

When are your meetings for today?

: ~ : •

: ~ : • _____

: ~ : • _____

: ~ : • _____

: ~ : •

Carry over tasks...

Overview
What does today look like?

: ~ : _____

: ~ : _____

: ~ : _____

: ~ : _____

: ~ : _____

: ~ : _____

: ~ : _____

: ~ : _____

: ~ : _____

: ~ : _____

: ~ : _____

: ~ : _____

What day is it?

List 3 things you are
grateful for...

- _____
- _____
- _____

List 3-10 tasks you must
accomplish today...

- _____
- _____
- _____
- _____
- _____
- _____
- _____
- _____
- _____
- _____

Schedule your meal times...

: ~ : •
_____
: ~ : •
_____
: ~ : •
_____
: ~ : •
_____
: ~ : •

Find 2 hours for metaphysics / belief
system development...

: ~ : •
_____
: ~ : •
_____
: ~ : •
_____
: ~ : •
_____
: ~ : •
_____
: ~ : •

Who do you appreciate today?

> *"Readjusting allows for more growth when spurred with new inspiration."*
> *- Ace Doligosa*

Schedule workouts...

1. 10-minute Cardio

_____

2. 10-minute Stretch

_____

3. 25-minute Activity

_____

Schedule work time...

When are your meetings for today?

:   ~   :   •
:   ~   :   • _____
:   ~   :   • _____
:   ~   :   • _____
:   ~   :   •

Carry over tasks...

Overview
What does today look like?

:   ~   :   _____
:   ~   :   _____
:   ~   :   _____
:   ~   :   _____
:   ~   :   _____
:   ~   :   _____
:   ~   :   _____
:   ~   :   _____
:   ~   :   _____
:   ~   :   _____
:   ~   :   _____
:   ~   :   _____

What day is it? _____

> *"And the more we open up to the universe, the more it opens to us."*
> *- GZA*

List 3 things you are grateful for...

- _____
- _____
- _____

List 3-10 tasks you must accomplish today...

- _____
- _____
- _____
- _____
- _____
- _____
- _____
- _____
- _____
- _____

Schedule your meal times...

: ~ : • _____
: ~ : • _____
: ~ : • _____
: ~ : • _____
: ~ : • _____

Find 2 hours for metaphysics / belief system development...

: ~ : • _____
: ~ : • _____
: ~ : • _____
: ~ : • _____
: ~ : • _____
: ~ : • _____

Who do you appreciate today?

> *"Good advice grates on the ear"*
> *- Proverb*

Schedule workouts...

1. 10-minute Cardio

_____

2. 10-minute Stretch

_____

3. 25-minute Activity

_____

Schedule work time...

When are your meetings for today?

: ~ : •

_____

: ~ : •

_____

: ~ : •

_____

: ~ : •

_____

: ~ : •

Carry over tasks...

Overview
What does today look like?

: ~ :

_____

: ~ :

_____

: ~ :

_____

: ~ :

_____

: ~ :

_____

: ~ :

_____

: ~ :

_____

: ~ :

_____

: ~ :

_____

: ~ :

_____

: ~ :

_____

: ~ :

_____

What day is it? ....

> *"Give me a lever, a fulcrum and a firm place to stand and I will move the world."*
> *- Archimedes*

List 3 things you are grateful for...

- _____
- _____
- _____

List 3-10 tasks you must accomplish today...

- _____
- _____
- _____
- _____
- _____
- _____
- _____
- _____
- _____
- _____

Schedule your meal times...

: ~ : • _____
: ~ : • _____
: ~ : • _____
: ~ : • _____
: ~ : • _____

Find 2 hours for metaphysics / belief system development...

: ~ : • _____
: ~ : • _____
: ~ : • _____
: ~ : • _____
: ~ : • _____
: ~ : • _____

Who do you appreciate today?

> *"Push through to completion."*
> *- Ray Dalio*

Schedule workouts...

1. 10-minute Cardio

_____

2. 10-minute Stretch

_____

3. 25-minute Activity

_____

Schedule work time...

When are your meetings for today?

: ~ : •

: ~ : • _____

: ~ : • _____

: ~ : • _____

: ~ : •

Carry over tasks...

Overview
What does today look like?

: ~ : _____

: ~ : _____

: ~ : _____

: ~ : _____

: ~ : _____

: ~ : _____

: ~ : _____

: ~ : _____

: ~ : _____

: ~ : _____

: ~ : _____

: ~ : _____

What day is it?

> *"Sometimes, you just have to play the role of a fool to fool the fool who thinks they are fooling you."*
> *- Unknown*

List 3 things you are grateful for...

- _____
- _____
- _____

List 3-10 tasks you must accomplish today...

- _____
- _____
- _____
- _____
- _____
- _____
- _____
- _____
- _____
- _____

Schedule your meal times...

: ~ : •
: ~ : •
: ~ : •
: ~ : •
: ~ : •

Find 2 hours for metaphysics / belief system development...

: ~ : •
: ~ : •
: ~ : •
: ~ : •
: ~ : •
: ~ : •

Who do you appreciate today?

> *"Cynicism is a choice. Hope is a better choice."*
> *- Barack Obama*

Schedule workouts...

1. 10-minute Cardio

_____

2. 10-minute Stretch

_____

3. 25-minute Activity

_____

Schedule work time...

When are your meetings for today?

: ~ : •
_____
: ~ : •
_____
: ~ : •
_____
: ~ : •
_____
: ~ : •

Carry over tasks...

Overview
What does today look like?

: ~ : _____

: ~ : _____

: ~ : _____

: ~ : _____

: ~ : _____

: ~ : _____

: ~ : _____

: ~ : _____

: ~ : _____

: ~ : _____

: ~ : _____

: ~ : _____

Weekly Plan

> *"As soon as you feel too old to do a thing, do it."*
> *- Margaret Dyland*

1. 45-Minute Daily conditioning workouts to keep you feeling sharp

SUN	MON	TUE	WED	THU	FRI	SAT

2. Plan 3 calls a day to feel grounded

SUN	MON	TUE	WED	THU	FRI	SAT

3. Plan 3 activities a week for fun

SUN	MON	TUE	WED	THU	FRI	SAT

Pro-tip:

Shonda Rhimes shared: "For one year, I would say yes to all the things that scared me. Anything that made me nervous, took me out of my comfort zone, I forced myself to say yes to. Did I want to speak in public? No, but yes. Did I want to be on live TV? No, but yes. Did I want to try acting?" Take this example and do the same, see how you your life expands when you do.

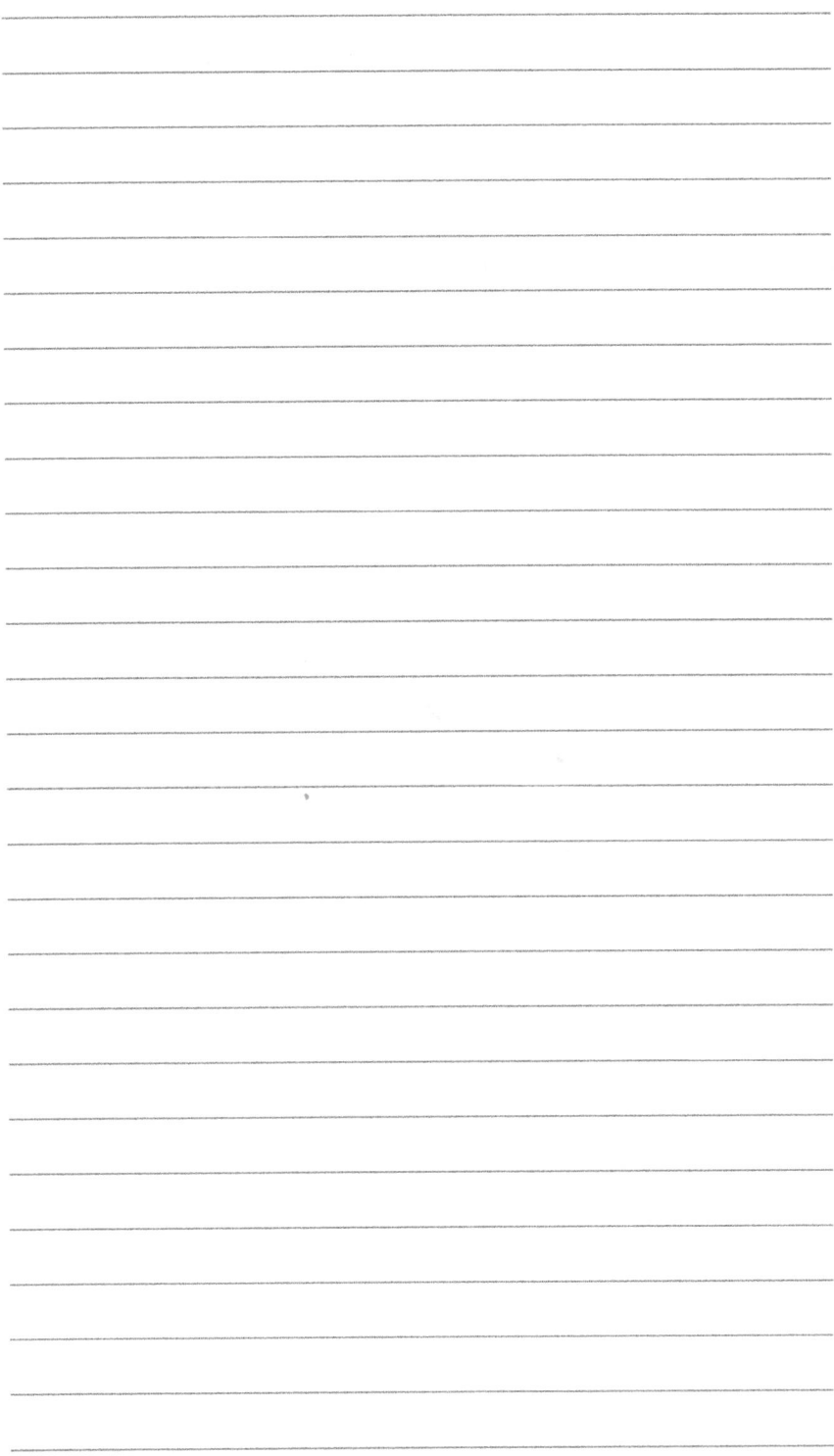

What day is it?

List 3 things you are grateful for...

- _____
- _____
- _____

List 3-10 tasks you must accomplish today...

- _____
- _____
- _____
- _____
- _____
- _____
- _____
- _____
- _____
- _____

Schedule your meal times...

: ~ : •
: ~ : •
: ~ : •
: ~ : •
: ~ : •

Find 2 hours for metaphysics / belief system development...

: ~ : •
: ~ : •
: ~ : •
: ~ : •
: ~ : •
: ~ : •

Who do you appreciate today?

> *"Be healthy and take care of yourself, but be happy with the beautiful things that make you, you. "*
> *- Beyonce*

Schedule workouts...

1. 10-minute Cardio

_____

2. 10-minute Stretch

_____

3. 25-minute Activity

_____

Schedule work time...

When are your meetings for today?

: ~ : •

: ~ : • _____

: ~ : • _____

: ~ : • _____

: ~ : •

Carry over tasks...

Overview
What does today look like?

: ~ : _____

: ~ : _____

: ~ : _____

: ~ : _____

: ~ : _____

: ~ : _____

: ~ : _____

: ~ : _____

: ~ : _____

: ~ : _____

: ~ : _____

What day is it? ....

> *"The best way to predict your future, is to create it."*
> *- Peter Drucker*

List 3 things you are
grateful for...

- _____
- _____
- _____

List 3-10 tasks you must
accomplish today...

- _____
- _____
- _____
- _____
- _____
- _____
- _____
- _____
- _____
- _____

Schedule your meal times...

- __:__ ~ __:__ •
- __:__ ~ __:__ •
- __:__ ~ __:__ •
- __:__ ~ __:__ •
- __:__ ~ __:__ •

Find 2 hours for metaphysics / belief
system development...

- __:__ ~ __:__ •
- __:__ ~ __:__ •
- __:__ ~ __:__ •
- __:__ ~ __:__ •
- __:__ ~ __:__ •
- __:__ ~ __:__ •

Who do you appreciate today?

> *"This is why we have two ears and only one mouth, that we may hear more and speak less."*
> *- Zenon*
> *(No, not Zenon in Girl of the 21st Century and, of course, don't forget the "zequel") but Zenon (Elea, 490 BCE) was a pre-Socratic Greek philosopher)*

Schedule workouts...

1. 10-minute Cardio

_____

2. 10-minute Stretch

_____

3. 25-minute Activity

_____

Schedule work time...

When are your meetings for today?

: ~ : •

: ~ : • _____

: ~ : • _____

: ~ : • _____

: ~ : • _____

Carry over tasks...

Overview
What does today look like?

: ~ : _____

: ~ : _____

: ~ : _____

: ~ : _____

: ~ : _____

: ~ : _____

: ~ : _____

: ~ : _____

: ~ : _____

: ~ : _____

: ~ : _____

: ~ : _____

: ~ : _____

What day is it?

List 3 things you are
grateful for...

Schedule your meal times...

- _____
- _____
- _____

: ~ : •

: ~ : •

: ~ : •

: ~ : •

: ~ : •

List 3-10 tasks you must
accomplish today...

- _____
- _____
- _____
- _____
- _____
- _____
- _____
- _____
- _____
- _____

Find 2 hours for metaphysics / belief
system development...

: ~ : •

: ~ : •

: ~ : •

: ~ : •

: ~ : •

: ~ : •

Who do you appreciate today?

> *"If you obey all the rules, you miss all the fun."*
> *- Katherine Hepburn*

Schedule workouts...

1. 10-minute Cardio

_____

2. 10-minute Stretch

_____

3. 25-minute Activity

_____

Schedule work time...

When are your meetings for today?

:   ~   :   •
_____
:   ~   :   •
_____
:   ~   :   •
_____
:   ~   :   •
_____
:   ~   :   •

Carry over tasks...

Overview
What does today look like?

:   ~   :
_____
:   ~   :
_____
:   ~   :
_____
:   ~   :
_____
:   ~   :
_____
:   ~   :
_____
:   ~   :
_____
:   ~   :
_____
:   ~   :
_____
:   ~   :
_____
:   ~   :
_____
:   ~   :
_____

What day is it?

List 3 things you are grateful for...

- _____
- _____
- _____

List 3-10 tasks you must accomplish today...

- _____
- _____
- _____
- _____
- _____
- _____
- _____
- _____
- _____

Schedule your meal times...

: ~ : •
: ~ : •
: ~ : •
: ~ : •
: ~ : •

Find 2 hours for metaphysics / belief system development...

: ~ : •
: ~ : •
: ~ : •
: ~ : •
: ~ : •
: ~ : •

Who do you appreciate today?

> *"Decision is the ultimate power. Decisions shapes destiny."*
> *- Tony Robbins*

Schedule workouts...

1. 10-minute Cardio

_____

2. 10-minute Stretch

_____

3. 25-minute Activity

_____

Schedule work time...

When are your meetings for today?

: ~ : •

: ~ : • _____

: ~ : • _____

: ~ : • _____

: ~ : •

Carry over tasks...

Overview
What does today look like?

: ~ :

: ~ :

: ~ :

: ~ :

: ~ :

: ~ :

: ~ :

: ~ :

: ~ :

: ~ :

: ~ :

: ~ :

What day is it?

> *"And at some point, all of us need to go out into the world to discover and to explore. That's the beginning of desire and create our exploratory needs, curiosity, discovery."*
> *- Esther Perel*

List 3 things you are grateful for...

- _____
- _____
- _____

List 3-10 tasks you must accomplish today...

- _____
- _____
- _____
- _____
- _____
- _____
- _____
- _____
- _____
- _____

Schedule your meal times...

- : ~ : •
- : ~ : •
- : ~ : •
- : ~ : •
- : ~ : •

Find 2 hours for metaphysics / belief system development...

- : ~ : •
- : ~ : •
- : ~ : •
- : ~ : •
- : ~ : •
- : ~ : •

Who do you appreciate today?

> *"The world is big, but it always fits in your heart. Take it with you always."*
> *- Xander Cage*

Schedule workouts...

1. 10-minute Cardio

_____

2. 10-minute Stretch

_____

3. 25-minute Activity

_____

Schedule work time...

When are your meetings for today?

: ~ : •

: ~ : •

: ~ : •

: ~ : •

: ~ : •

Carry over tasks...

Overview
What does today look like?

: ~ :

: ~ :

: ~ :

: ~ :

: ~ :

: ~ :

: ~ :

: ~ :

: ~ :

: ~ :

: ~ :

: ~ :

: ~ :

What day is it?

List 3 things you are grateful for...

- _____
- _____
- _____

List 3-10 tasks you must accomplish today...

- _____
- _____
- _____
- _____
- _____
- _____
- _____
- _____
- _____
- _____

Schedule your meal times...

:   ~   :   •   _____

:   ~   :   •   _____

:   ~   :   •   _____

:   ~   :   •   _____

:   ~   :   •   _____

Find 2 hours for metaphysics / belief system development...

:   ~   :   •   _____

:   ~   :   •   _____

:   ~   :   •   _____

:   ~   :   •   _____

:   ~   :   •   _____

:   ~   :   •   _____

Who do you appreciate today?

Schedule workouts...

1. 10-minute Cardio

_____

2. 10-minute Stretch

_____

3. 25-minute Activity

_____

Schedule work time...

When are your meetings for today?

: ~ : •

: ~ : • _____

: ~ : • _____

: ~ : • _____

: ~ : • _____

Carry over tasks...

Overview
What does today look like?

: ~ : _____

: ~ : _____

: ~ : _____

: ~ : _____

: ~ : _____

: ~ : _____

: ~ : _____

: ~ : _____

: ~ : _____

: ~ : _____

: ~ : _____

: ~ : _____

: ~ : _____

What day is it?

List 3 things you are grateful for...

- _____
- _____
- _____

List 3-10 tasks you must accomplish today...

- _____
- _____
- _____
- _____
- _____
- _____
- _____
- _____
- _____
- _____

Schedule your meal times...

:   ~   :   •
:   ~   :   •
:   ~   :   •
:   ~   :   •
:   ~   :   •

Find 2 hours for metaphysics / belief system development...

:   ~   :   •
:   ~   :   •
:   ~   :   •
:   ~   :   •
:   ~   :   •
:   ~   :   •

Who do you appreciate today?

> *"When I was young, I lived in two worlds. Outside my house was America. Inside my house was the Philippines. No matter where I was, it was a fight to be me."*
> *- Ace Doligosa*

Schedule workouts...

1. 10-minute Cardio

_____

2. 10-minute Stretch

_____

3. 25-minute Activity

_____

Schedule work time...

When are your meetings for today?

: ~ : •

: ~ : • _____

: ~ : • _____

: ~ : • _____

: ~ : •

Carry over tasks...

Overview
What does today look like?

: ~ :

: ~ :

: ~ :

: ~ :

: ~ :

: ~ :

: ~ :

: ~ :

: ~ :

: ~ :

: ~ :

: ~ :

Weekly Plan

> *"Success is not final, failure is not fatal: it is the courage to continue that counts."*
>
> *- Winston Churchill*

1. 45-Minute Daily conditioning workouts to keep you feeling sharp

SUN	MON	TUE	WED	THU	FRI	SAT

2. Plan 3 calls a day to feel grounded

SUN	MON	TUE	WED	THU	FRI	SAT

3. Plan 3 activities a week for fun

SUN	MON	TUE	WED	THU	FRI	SAT

Pro-tip: *What is it that you believe people are thinking about you? Write that down..*

Finished? Great, now rip up that note and throw it in the trash. It's not real.
Now take a fresh page and write down what kind of person you want to be. List your characteristics and qualities in affirmations.
Like "I am smart", "I am strong," "I am beautiful," "I am good." "I can overcome anything." "I have strong integrity, loyalty, strength, courage, and compassionate etc."
Great - Words are powerful.
Now repeat this out loud three times - "I am who I choose to be."
Wonderful - this is who you are.

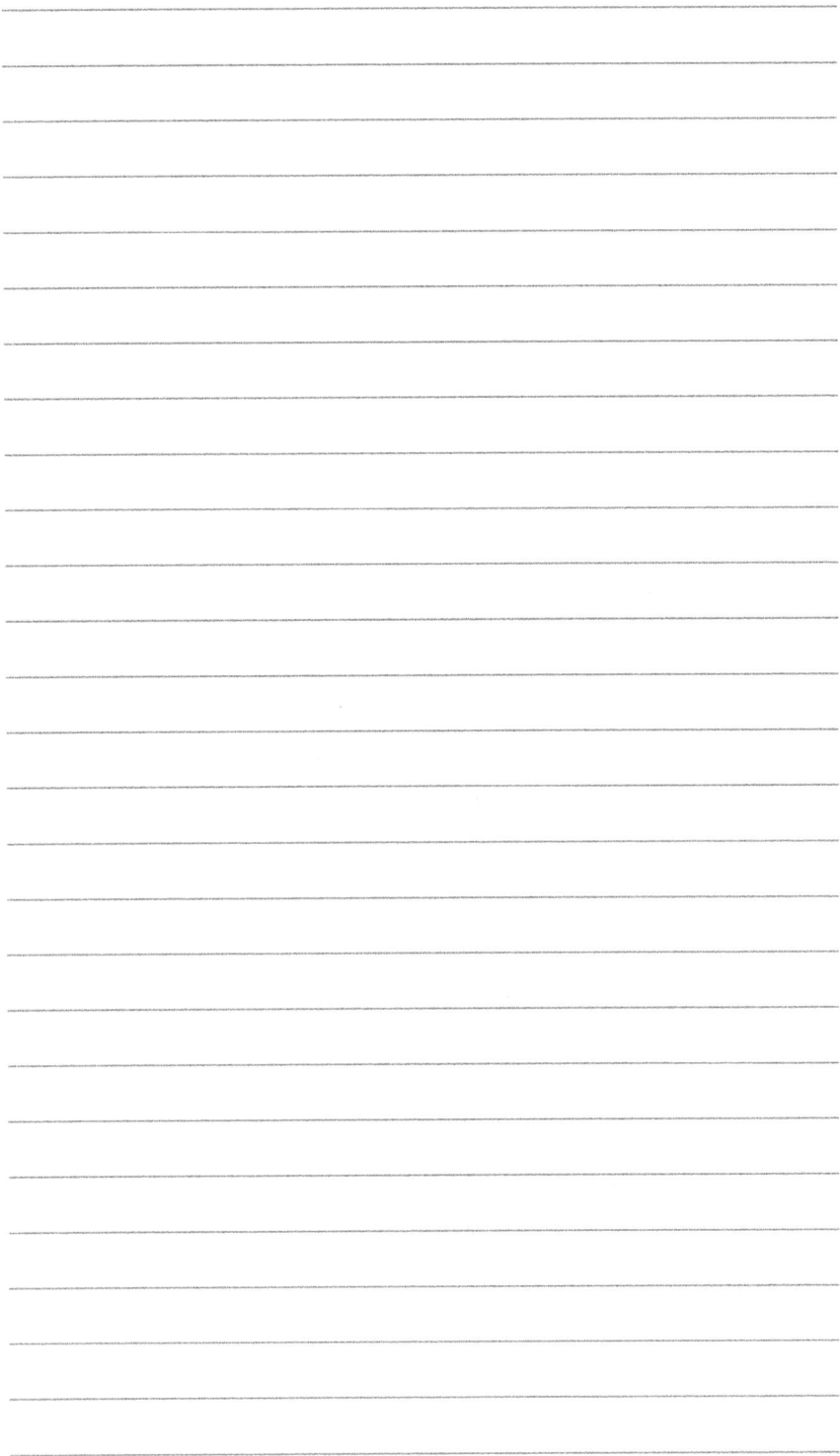

What day is it?

List 3 things you are grateful for...

- _____
- _____
- _____

List 3-10 tasks you must accomplish today...

- _____
- _____
- _____
- _____
- _____
- _____
- _____
- _____
- _____
- _____

Schedule your meal times...

```
:   ~   :   •   _____
:   ~   :   •   _____
:   ~   :   •   _____
:   ~   :   •   _____
:   ~   :   •   _____
```

Find 2 hours for metaphysics / belief system development...

```
:   ~   :   •   _____
:   ~   :   •   _____
:   ~   :   •   _____
:   ~   :   •   _____
:   ~   :   •   _____
:   ~   :   •   _____
```

Who do you appreciate today?

> *"Like all great art, it defies the tyrant Time."*
> *- Edwin A. Abbott*

Schedule workouts...

1. 10-minute Cardio

_____

2. 10-minute Stretch

_____

3. 25-minute Activity

_____

Schedule work time...

When are your meetings for today?

: ~ : •
: ~ : • _____
: ~ : • _____
: ~ : • _____
: ~ : • _____

Carry over tasks...

Overview
What does today look like?

: ~ : _____
: ~ : _____
: ~ : _____
: ~ : _____
: ~ : _____
: ~ : _____
: ~ : _____
: ~ : _____
: ~ : _____
: ~ : _____
: ~ : _____
: ~ : _____

What day is it? _____

> "The starting point of all achievement is DESIRE. Keep this constantly in mind. Weak desire brings weak results, just as a small fire makes a small amount of heat."
> - Napoleon Hill

List 3 things you are grateful for...

- _____
- _____
- _____

List 3-10 tasks you must accomplish today...

- _____
- _____
- _____
- _____
- _____
- _____
- _____
- _____
- _____
- _____

Schedule your meal times...

:	~	:	•
:	~	:	•
:	~	:	•
:	~	:	•
:	~	:	•

Find 2 hours for metaphysics / belief system development...

:	~	:	•
:	~	:	•
:	~	:	•
:	~	:	•
:	~	:	•
:	~	:	•

Who do you appreciate today?

> *"Those who think they have no time for bodily exercise will sooner or later have to find time for illness."*
> *- Edward Stanley*

Schedule workouts...

1. 10-minute Cardio

_____

2. 10-minute Stretch

_____

3. 25-minute Activity

_____

Schedule work time...

When are your meetings for today?

: ~ : •

: ~ : • _____

: ~ : • _____

: ~ : • _____

: ~ : •

Carry over tasks...

Overview
What does today look like?

: ~ : _____

: ~ : _____
        _____

: ~ : _____
        _____

: ~ : _____
        _____

: ~ : _____
        _____

: ~ : _____
        _____

: ~ : _____
        _____

: ~ : _____
        _____

: ~ : _____
        _____

: ~ : _____
        _____

: ~ : _____
        _____

: ~ : _____

What day is it? ....

> *"If you set your goals ridiculously high and it's a failure—you will fail above everyone else's success."*
> *- James Cameron*

List 3 things you are grateful for...

- _____
- _____
- _____

List 3-10 tasks you must accomplish today...

- _____
- _____
- _____
- _____
- _____
- _____
- _____
- _____
- _____
- _____

Schedule your meal times...

: ~ : •
: ~ : •
: ~ : •
: ~ : •
: ~ : •

Find 2 hours for metaphysics / belief system development...

: ~ : •
: ~ : •
: ~ : •
: ~ : •
: ~ : •
: ~ : •

Who do you appreciate today?

> *"At the end of the day, we have two things in common: we all don't want to suffer and we all want to be happy."*
> *- Ace Doligosa*

Schedule workouts...

1. 10-minute Cardio

_____

2. 10-minute Stretch

_____

3. 25-minute Activity

_____

Schedule work time...

When are your meetings for today?

```
:   ~   :   •
:   ~   :   •   _____
:   ~   :   •   _____
:   ~   :   •   _____
:   ~   :   •
```

Carry over tasks...

Overview
What does today look like?

```
:   ~   :   _____
:   ~   :   _____
:   ~   :   _____
:   ~   :   _____
:   ~   :   _____
:   ~   :   _____
:   ~   :   _____
:   ~   :   _____
:   ~   :   _____
:   ~   :   _____
:   ~   :   _____
:   ~   :   _____
```

What day is it?

List 3 things you are grateful for...

- _____
- _____
- _____

List 3-10 tasks you must accomplish today...

- _____
- _____
- _____
- _____
- _____
- _____
- _____
- _____
- _____
- _____

Schedule your meal times...

:   ~   :   • _____
:   ~   :   • _____
:   ~   :   • _____
:   ~   :   • _____
:   ~   :   • _____

Find 2 hours for metaphysics / belief system development...

:   ~   :   • _____
:   ~   :   • _____
:   ~   :   • _____
:   ~   :   • _____
:   ~   :   • _____
:   ~   :   • _____

Who do you appreciate today?

¹(Black humor definition: a form of humor that regards human suffering as absurd rather than pitiable)

> *"There are some things in life that we desperately want to change, and we cannot."*
> *- Kathryn Schulz*

Schedule workouts...

1. 10-minute Cardio

_____

2. 10-minute Stretch

_____

3. 25-minute Activity

_____

Schedule work time...

When are your meetings for today?

```
:   ~   :      •
:   ~   :      •  _____
:   ~   :      •
:   ~   :      •  _____
:   ~   :      •
```

Carry over tasks...

Overview
What does today look like?

```
:    ~    :    _____
:    ~    :    _____
:    ~    :    _____
:    ~    :    _____
:    ~    :    _____
:    ~    :    _____
:    ~    :    _____
:    ~    :    _____
:    ~    :    _____
:    ~    :    _____
:    ~    :    _____
:    ~    :    _____
```

What day is it? ....

> *"Listen. I wish I could tell you it gets better. But, it doesn't get better. You get better."*
> *- Joan Rivers*

List 3 things you are grateful for...

- _____
- _____
- _____

List 3-10 tasks you must accomplish today...

- _____
- _____
- _____
- _____
- _____
- _____
- _____
- _____
- _____
- _____

Schedule your meal times...

: ~ : • _____
: ~ : • _____
: ~ : • _____
: ~ : • _____
: ~ : • _____

Find 2 hours for metaphysics / belief system development...

: ~ : • _____
: ~ : • _____
: ~ : • _____
: ~ : • _____
: ~ : • _____
: ~ : • _____

Who do you appreciate today?

Schedule workouts...

1. 10-minute Cardio

_____

2. 10-minute Stretch

_____

3. 25-minute Activity

_____

Schedule work time...

When are your meetings for today?

: ~ : •

: ~ : • _____

: ~ : • _____

: ~ : • _____

: ~ : •

Carry over tasks...

Overview
What does today look like?

: ~ : _____

: ~ : _____

: ~ : _____

: ~ : _____

: ~ : _____

: ~ : _____

: ~ : _____

: ~ : _____

: ~ : _____

: ~ : _____

: ~ : _____

: ~ : _____

What day is it? _____

> *"If you're hurting, it is difficult. It is a battle within your own mind, and you have to be diligent to win but you do have weapons, you can fight, and you will heal."*
> *- Guy Winch*

List 3 things you are grateful for...

• _____
• _____
• _____

List 3-10 tasks you must accomplish today...

• _____
• _____
• _____
• _____
• _____
• _____
• _____
• _____
• _____
• _____

Schedule your meal times...

__ : __ ~ __ : __ • _____
__ : __ ~ __ : __ • _____
__ : __ ~ __ : __ • _____
__ : __ ~ __ : __ • _____
__ : __ ~ __ : __ • _____

Find 2 hours for metaphysics / belief system development...

__ : __ ~ __ : __ • _____
__ : __ ~ __ : __ • _____
__ : __ ~ __ : __ • _____
__ : __ ~ __ : __ • _____
__ : __ ~ __ : __ • _____
__ : __ ~ __ : __ • _____

Who do you appreciate today?

Schedule workouts...

1. 10-minute Cardio

_____

2. 10-minute Stretch

_____

3. 25-minute Activity

_____

Schedule work time...

When are your meetings for today?

:   ~   :   •
:   ~   :   • _____
:   ~   :   • _____
:   ~   :   • _____
:   ~   :   • _____

Carry over tasks...

Overview
What does today look like?

:   ~   :   _____
:   ~   :   _____
:   ~   :   _____
:   ~   :   _____
:   ~   :   _____
:   ~   :   _____
:   ~   :   _____
:   ~   :   _____
:   ~   :   _____
:   ~   :   _____
:   ~   :   _____
:   ~   :   _____

What day is it?

List 3 things you are grateful for...

- _____
- _____
- _____

List 3-10 tasks you must accomplish today...

- _____
- _____
- _____
- _____
- _____
- _____
- _____
- _____
- _____
- _____

Schedule your meal times...

```
:     ~    :    •
:     ~    :    •
:     ~    :    •
:     ~    :    •
:     ~    :    •
```

Find 2 hours for metaphysics / belief system development...

```
:     ~    :    •
:     ~    :    •
:     ~    :    •
:     ~    :    •
:     ~    :    •
:     ~    :    •
```

Who do you appreciate today?

> *"My mother had a saying: Kamala, you may be the first to do many things, but make sure you're not the last."*
> *- Kamala Harris*

Schedule workouts...

1. 10-minute Cardio

_____

2. 10-minute Stretch

_____

3. 25-minute Activity

_____

Schedule work time...

When are your meetings for today?

```
:   ~   :   •
:   ~   :   • _____
:   ~   :   • _____
:   ~   :   • _____
:   ~   :   •
```

Carry over tasks...

Overview
What does today look like?

```
:   ~   :   _____
:   ~   :   _____
:   ~   :   _____
:   ~   :   _____
:   ~   :   _____
:   ~   :   _____
:   ~   :   _____
:   ~   :   _____
:   ~   :   _____
:   ~   :   _____
:   ~   :   _____
:   ~   :   _____
```

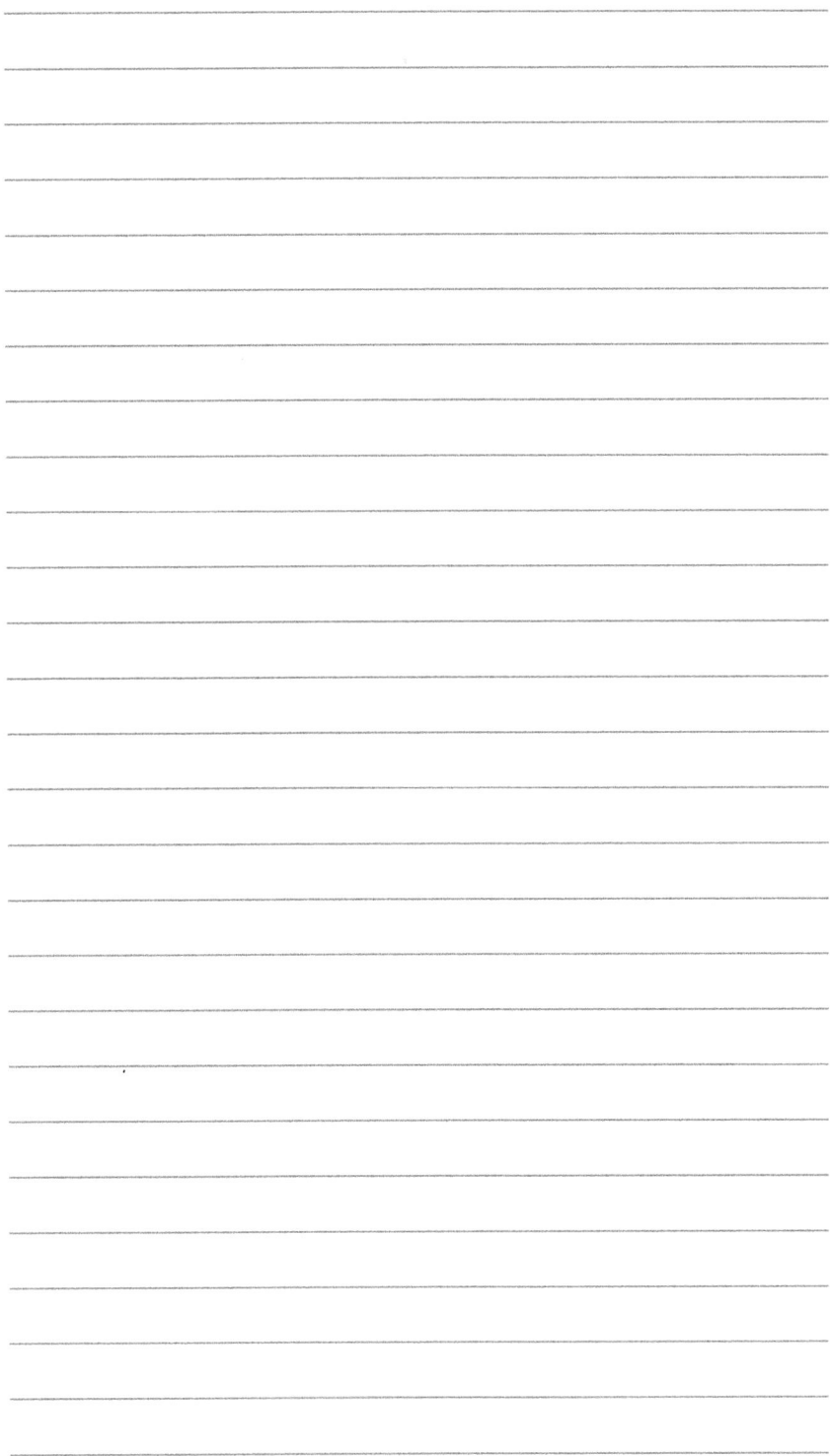

About the Author

Ace Doligosa was born on August 26th, 1992 in Manhattan, New York and lived in Edison, New Jersey until she was 18 years old. As the youngest of five siblings, she is the second to graduate college with a Bachelors in Communications at St. John's University. Since then, she has sustained strong relationships in media, entertainment, politics, technology, and entrepreneurialism.

Notable executives, producers, and public figures she has worked with include Susan Jin Davis, Sallie Schoneboom, Cubby Bryant, and Alex Ditrolio, many of whom work or worked at companies such as iHeartRadio, SiriusXM, Comcast NBCUniversal Inc. and CAA.

At an early age, Ace had thoughts of suicide and found that suicidal thoughts were not uncommon amongst her communities. Throughout her experiences, she found that she was not alone in her struggles. In 2017, TIME Magazine reported that public-health groups discovered that 36,000 millennials died due to "deaths of despair." As a minority millennial who overcame adversity from discrimination, public mental health negligence, immigration challenges, and financial obstacles, she now serves as an Artist, Mental Health Awareness Advocate, and Entrepreneur.

www.ingramcontent.com/pod-product-compliance
Lightning Source LLC
Chambersburg PA
CBHW070439100426
42812CB00031B/3340/J